GREAT MINDS® WIT & WISDOM

Grade 1 Module 1
A World of Books

Student Edition

GREAT MINDS

Great Minds® is the creator of *Eureka Math*®,
Wit & Wisdom®, *Alexandria Plan*™, and *PhD Science*®.

Published by Great Minds PBC
greatminds.org

© 2023 Great Minds PBC. All rights reserved. No part of this work may be reproduced or used in any form or by any means—graphic, electronic, or mechanical, including photocopying or information storage and retrieval systems—without written permission from the copyright holder.

1 2 3 4 5 6 7 8 9 10 QMX 27 26 25 24 23
Printed in Mexico
979-8-88588-718-2

STUDENT EDITION

Handout 1A: Notice and Wonder Prompt Cards

Handout 3A: Tomás Sentence Frame

Handout 3B: Nouns Chart

Handout 4A: Focusing Question 1 Prompt

Handout 4B: Noun Cards

Handout 5A: Frayer Model

Handout 6A: Essential Questions Chart

Handout 6B: Frayer Model

Handout 7A: Fluency Homework

Handout 9A: Past Tense

Handout 11A: Focusing Question 2 Prompt

Handout 11B: Frayer Model

Handout 13A: Fluency Homework/Evaluation

Handout 14A: Frayer Model

Handout 15A: Nouns

Handout 15B: Frayer Model

Handout 16A: Focusing Question 3 Prompt

Handout 17A: Fluency Homework

Handout 18A: Story Map

Handout 18B: Multiple-Meaning Words

Handout 19A: Frayer Model

Handout 21A: Focusing Question Task 4

Handout 22A: Adding Adjectives to Nouns

Handout 23A: New-Read Story Map

Handout 23B: Fluency Homework

Handout 23C: Mixed Sentences

Handout 24A: Art Vocabulary

Handout 25A: Sequenced Sentences

Handout 25B: Mixed Sentences

Handout 26A: Focusing Question Task 5

Handout 28A: End-of-Module Task

Handout 28B: Fluency Homework

Handout 29A: Narrative Checklist

Handout 32A: Socratic Seminar Self-Reflection

Volume of Reading Reflection Questions

Wit & Wisdom Family Tip Sheet

G1 > M1 > Handout 1A • WIT & WISDOM®

Name:

Handout 1A:
Notice and Wonder Prompt Cards

Directions: Cut out the Notice and Wonder Prompt Cards. Use them as you notice and wonder about a text.

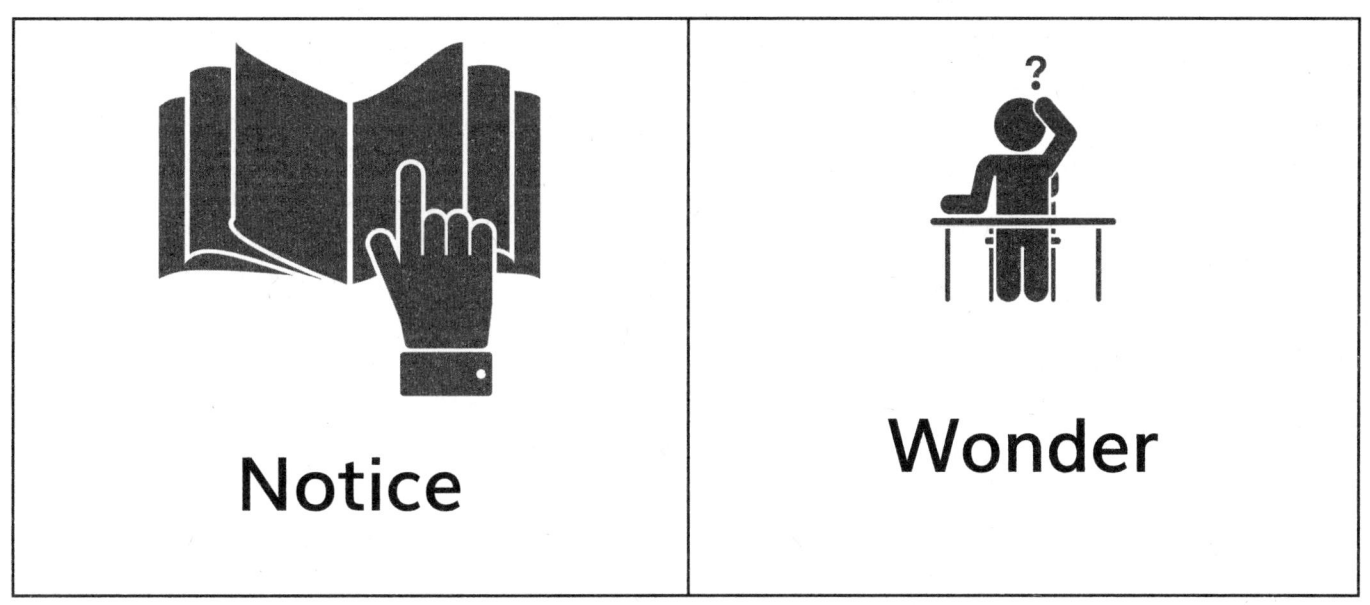

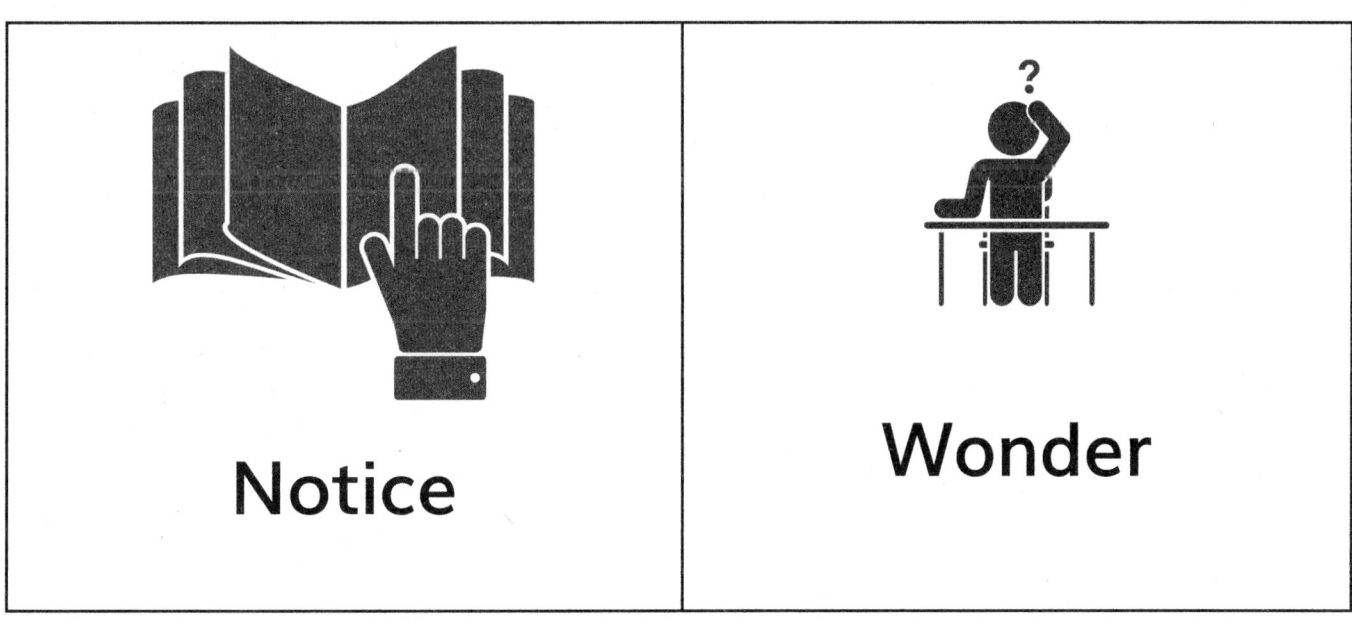

Notice	Wonder
Notice	Wonder

Handout 3A: Tomás Sentence Frame

Directions: Write and illustrate to describe one setting in *Tomás and the Library Lady*.

Tomás went to _____

Name: _____

Handout 3B: Nouns Chart

Directions: Write the nouns from the class Nouns Chart and place in Response Journal.

Nouns		
Common Nouns ("the ___")	People (characters)	
	Places (settings)	
	Things	
Proper Nouns		

Name: _____

Handout 4A:
Focusing Question 1 Prompt

Directions: Write and draw to retell the story *Tomás and the Library Lady*.

Be sure to include:

- Characters
- Setting
- Problem
- Resolution

Handout 4B: Noun Cards

Name: _____

Directions: Cut out the noun cards and use them to sort into common and proper nouns on the following chart.

Ben	Tomás	ball
Papá	book	car

Name:

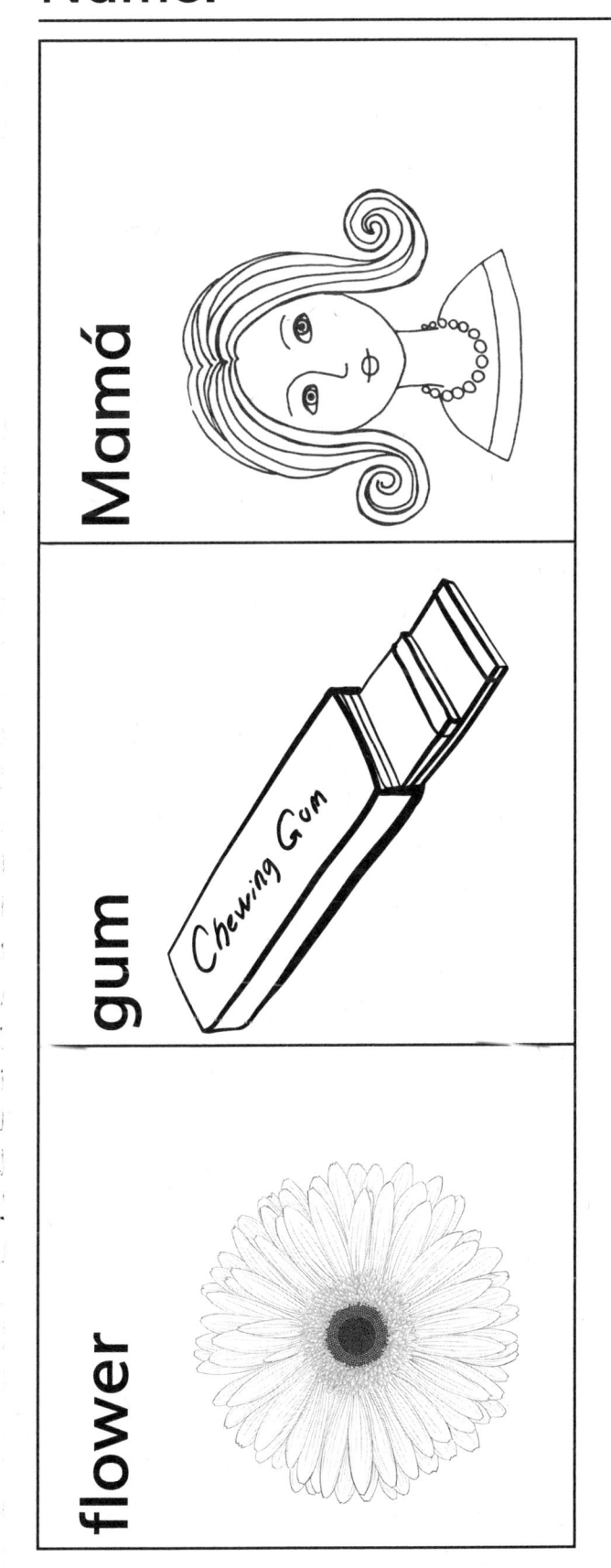

Mamá

gum

flower

Name:

Nouns	Proper Nouns	
	Common Nouns	

Name:

Handout 5A: Frayer Model

Directions: Fill in the information about the word *imagination* on the Frayer Model.

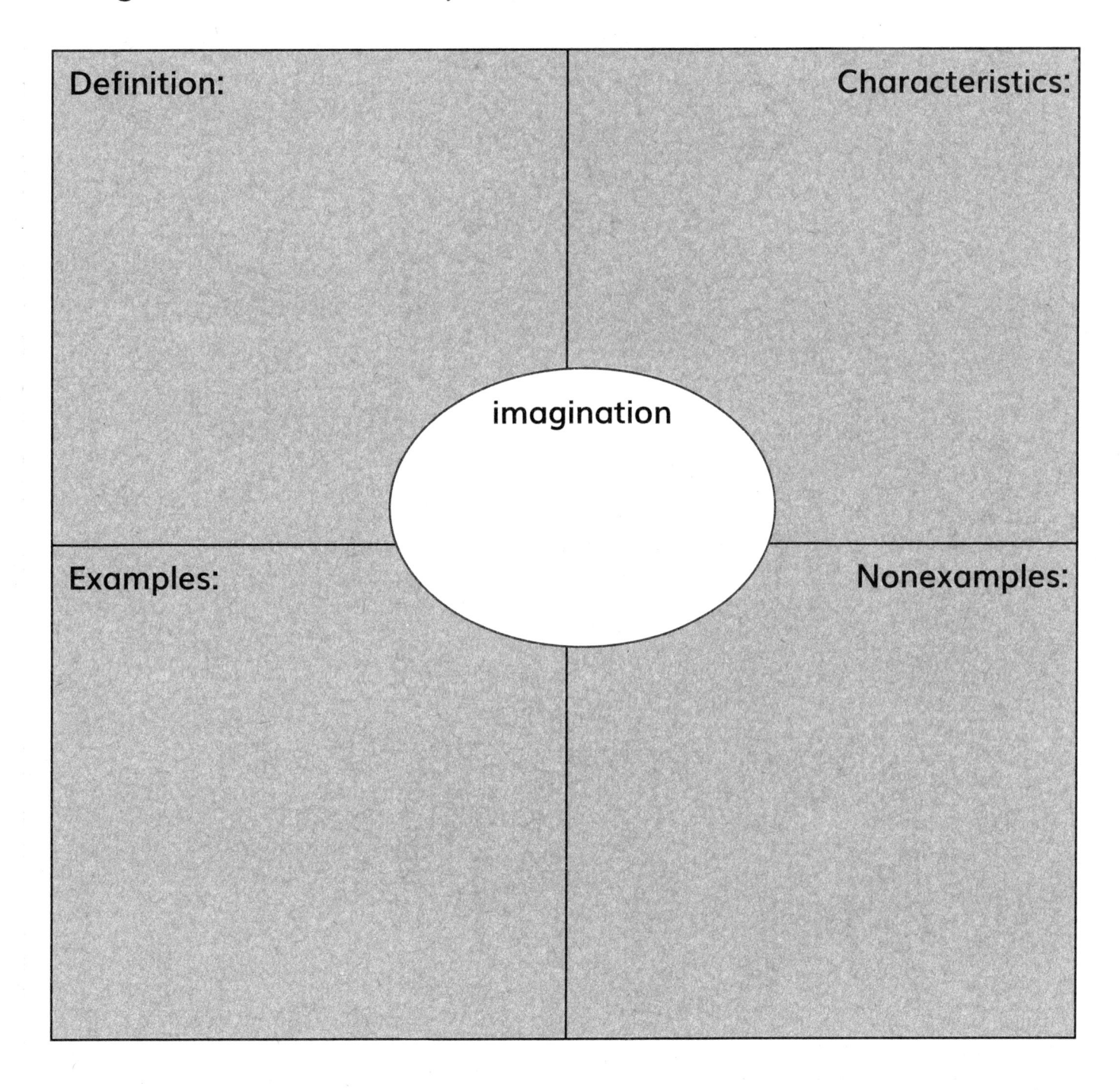

Definition:	Characteristics:
Examples:	Nonexamples:

imagination

Handout 6A: Essential Questions Chart

Directions: Write and illustrate to complete the chart using information from *Tomás and the Library Lady*, *Waiting for the Biblioburro*, and *That Book Woman*. Use one page for each story.

Essential Question: *How do books change people's lives around the world?*

Main Character	Where in the world is this character?	How do books change the character's life?

Name:

Essential Question: *How do books change people's lives around the world?*

How do books change the character's life?	
Where in the world is this character?	
Main Character	

Name:

Essential Question: How do books change people's lives around the world?

Main Character	
Where in the world is this character?	
How do books change the character's life?	

Name:

Handout 6B: Frayer Model

Directions: Fill in the information about the word *value* on the Frayer Model.

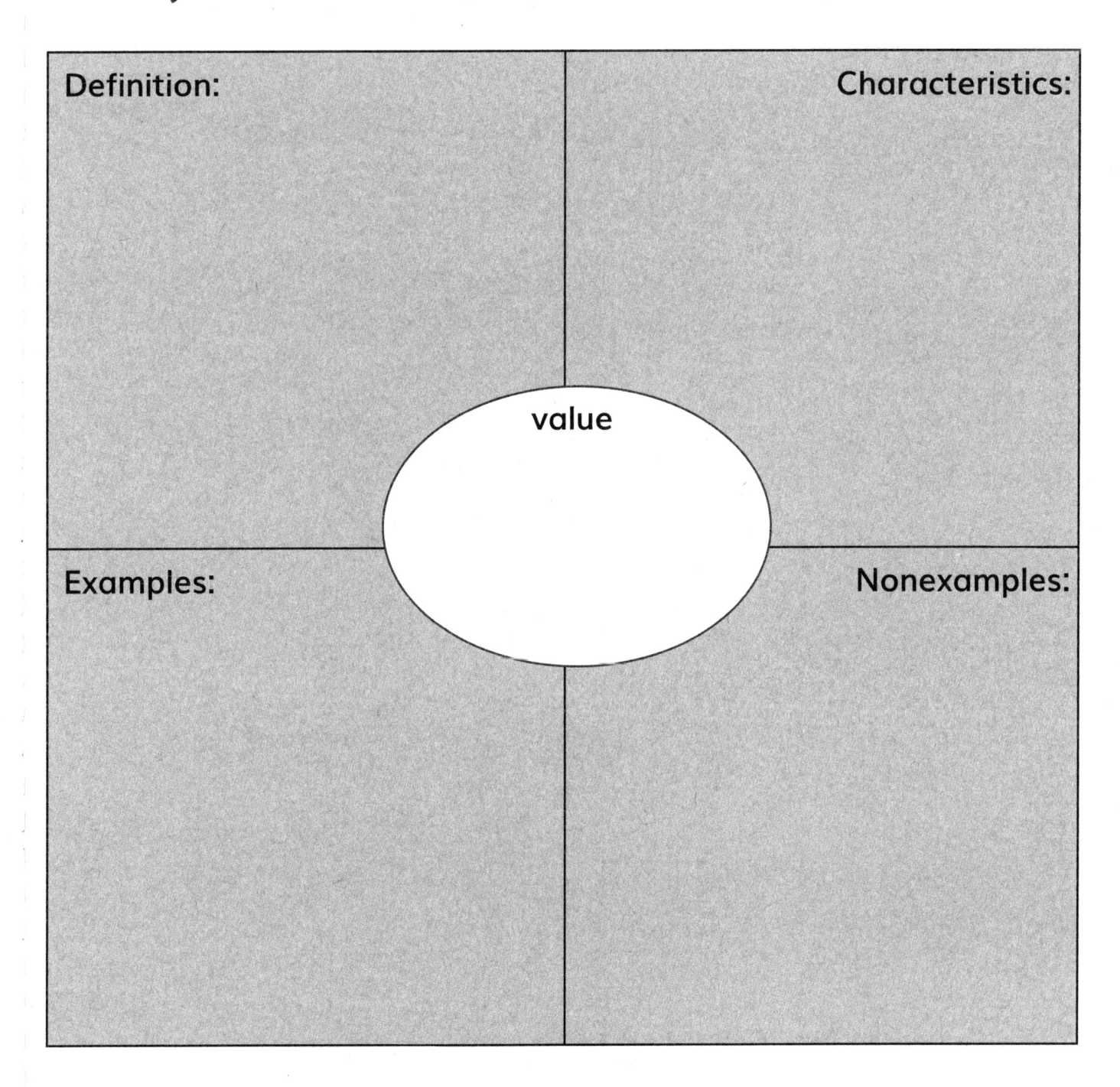

Definition:	Characteristics:
Examples:	Nonexamples:

value

Name:

Handout 7A: Fluency Homework

Directions: Have an adult initial each day that you read the passage three to five times. Optional: Have a peer sign on the second row of boxes, checking your progress below.

"Someone should write a story about your burros," Ana tells the librarian, rubbing Alfa's nose and feeding more grass to Beto.

"Why don't you?" he asks. Then he packs up the books and is off.

"Enjoy!" he calls to the children. "I will be back."

45 words

Brown, Monica. *Waiting for the Biblioburro*. Random House, 2011.

Day 1	Day 2	Day 3	Day 4	Day 5	Day 6

Name:

Student Performance Checklist:

- Read easily without stumbling.

- Read with appropriate phrasing and pausing.

- Read with appropriate expression for the selection.

- Read at a good pace, not too fast and not too slow.

- Read to be heard and understood.

Teacher Notes:

Name:

Handout 9A: Past Tense

Directions: Cut out the word cards and the endings. Add the endings to the word cards to make the verbs past tense.

talk	move	jump
lock	look	help
pick	imagine	bake

ed	ed	ed
ed	ed	ed
ed	ed	ed

Name: _____

Handout 11A:
Focusing Question 2 Prompt

Directions: Write and draw to retell the story *Waiting for the Biblioburro*.

Be sure to include:

- Characters
- Setting
- Problem
- Resolution

Name:

- Complete sentences

- End punctuation

Name:

Handout 11B: Frayer Model

Directions: Fill in the information about the word *inspire* on the Frayer Model.

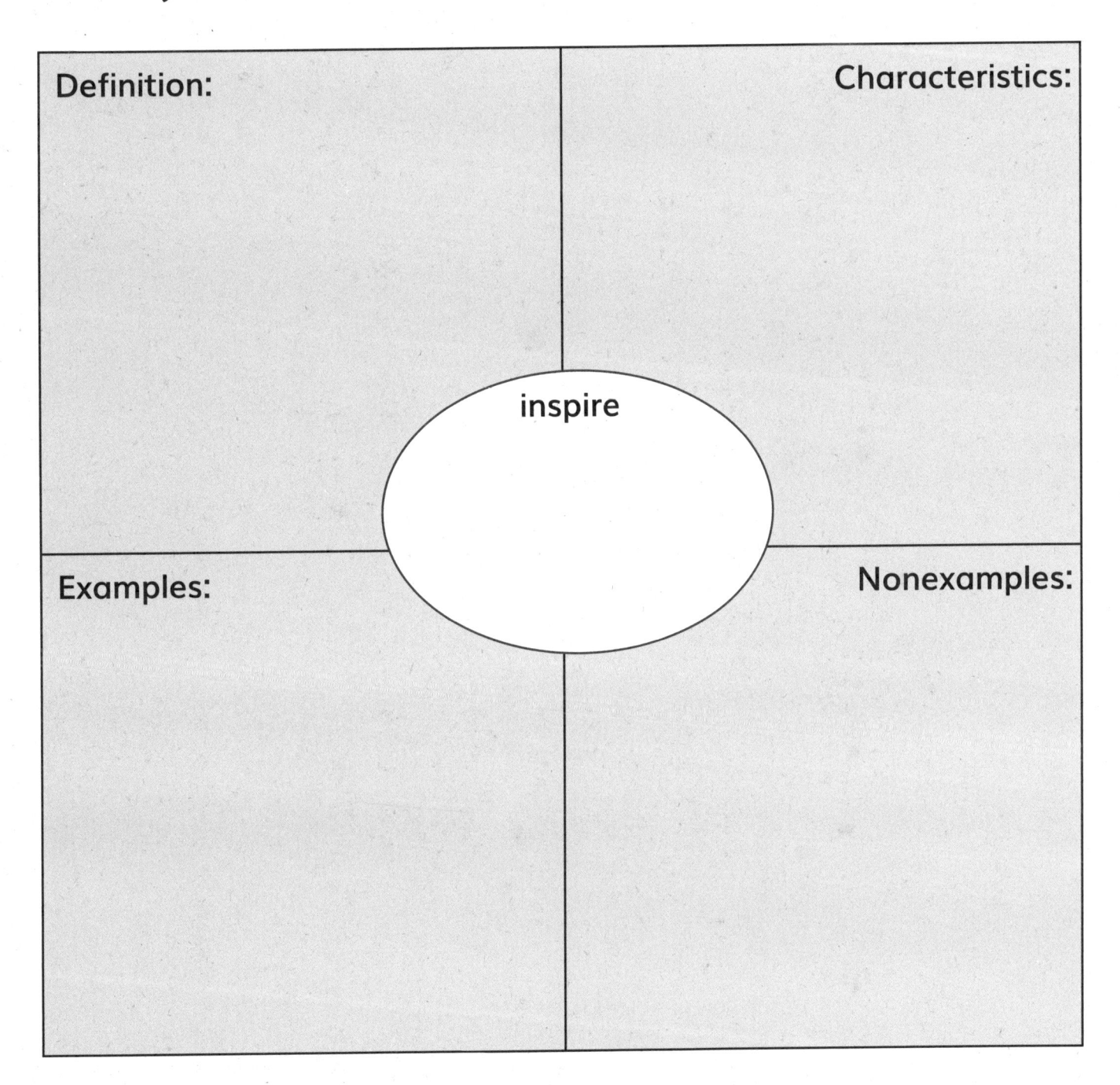

Definition:	Characteristics:
Examples:	Nonexamples:

inspire

Name:

Handout 13A:
Fluency Homework/Evaluation

Directions: Have an adult initial each day that you read the poem three to five times. Optional: Have a peer sign on the second row of boxes, checking your progress below.

"Museum AB—See!"

"A is for Apple"—I see red, green, gold.
"B is for Boat"—I see lines so bold!
"C is for Cat"—I see fuzzy friends.
"D is for Dance"—I see leaps and bends.
"E is for Egg"—I see ovals round.
"F is for Feet"—I see toes on the ground.

49 words

Adapted from The Metropolitan Museum of Art. *Museum ABC*. Little, Brown Books for Young Readers, 2002.

Day 1	Day 2	Day 3	Day 4

Name:

Student Performance Checklist:

- Read easily without stumbling.

- Read with appropriate phrasing and pausing.

- Read with appropriate expression for the selection.

- Read at a good pace, not too fast and not too slow.

- Read to be heard and understood.

Teacher Notes:

Name:

Handout 14A: Frayer Model

Directions: Fill in the information about the word *remote* on the Frayer Model.

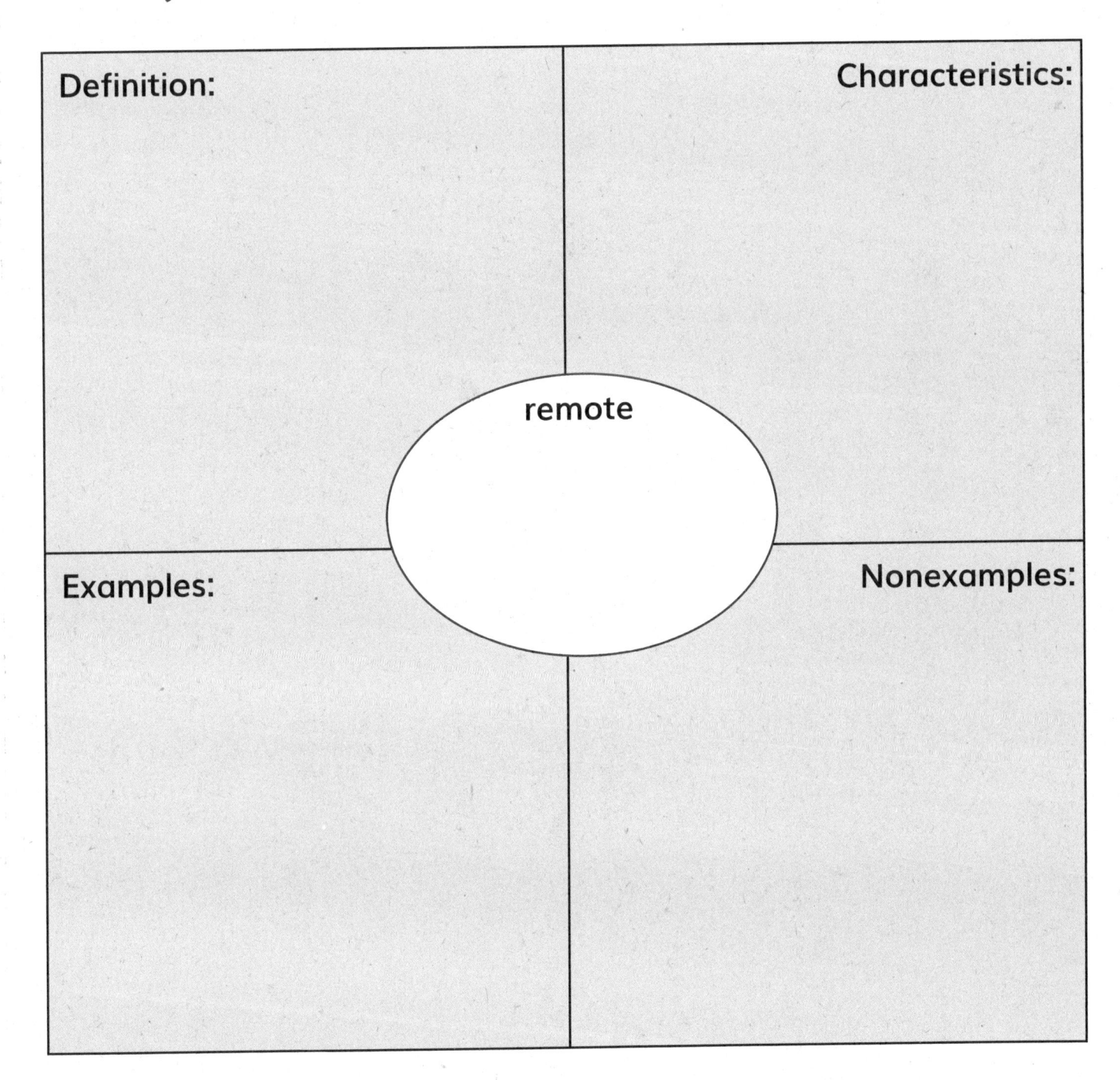

Definition:	Characteristics:
Examples:	Nonexamples:

remote

Name:

Handout 15A: Nouns

Directions: Cut apart the word cards. Place them in front of you so you can read each card.

England	england	wheelbarrow
kenya	camel	Kenya
donkey cart	peru	Peru

Name:

Handout 15B: Frayer Model

Directions: Fill in the information about the word *mobile* on the Frayer Model.

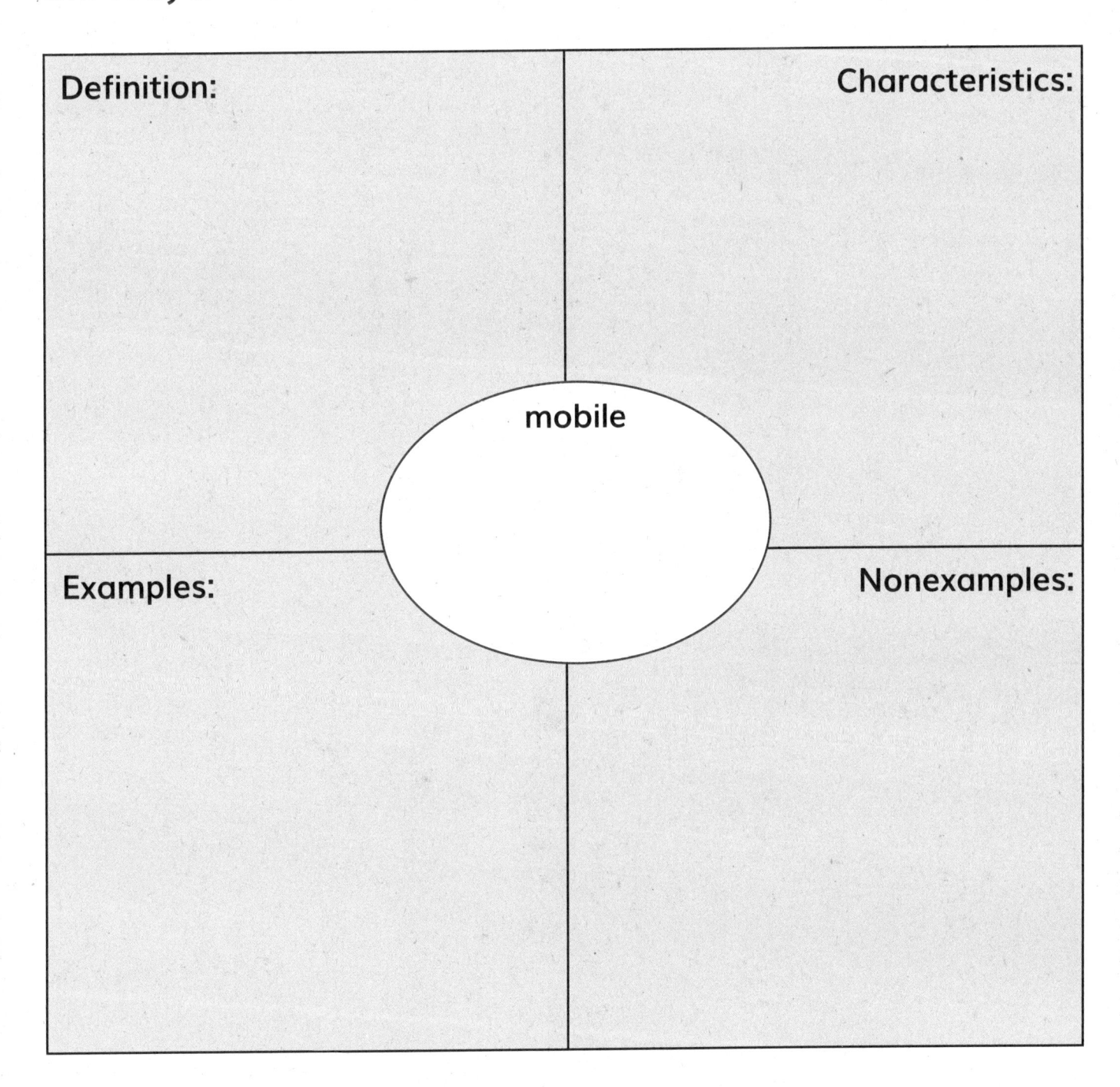

Definition:	Characteristics:
Examples:	Nonexamples:

mobile

Name: _____

Handout 16A:
Focusing Question 3 Prompt

Directions: Describe how children get books in your section of *My Librarian Is a Camel* by answering the question: "Using evidence from the photographs, how do people in this country get books?"

Be sure to:

- Write complete sentences.

- Capitalize proper nouns.

- Use end punctuation.

Name:

Handout 17A: Fluency Homework

Directions: Have an adult initial each day that you read the passage three to five times. Optional: Have a peer sign on the second row of boxes, checking your progress below.

I pick a book with words
and pictures, too,
and hold it out.
"Teach me what it says."
And Lark,
she does not laugh
or even tease, but makes a place,
and quiet-like,
we start to read.

37 words

Henson, Heather. *That Book Woman*. Atheneum Books for Young Readers, 2008.

Day 1	Day 2	Day 3	Day 4

Name:

Student Performance Checklist:

- Read easily without stumbling.

- Read with appropriate phrasing and pausing.

- Read with appropriate expression for the selection.

- Read at a good pace, not too fast and not too slow.

- Read to be heard and understood.

Teacher Notes:

Name: _____

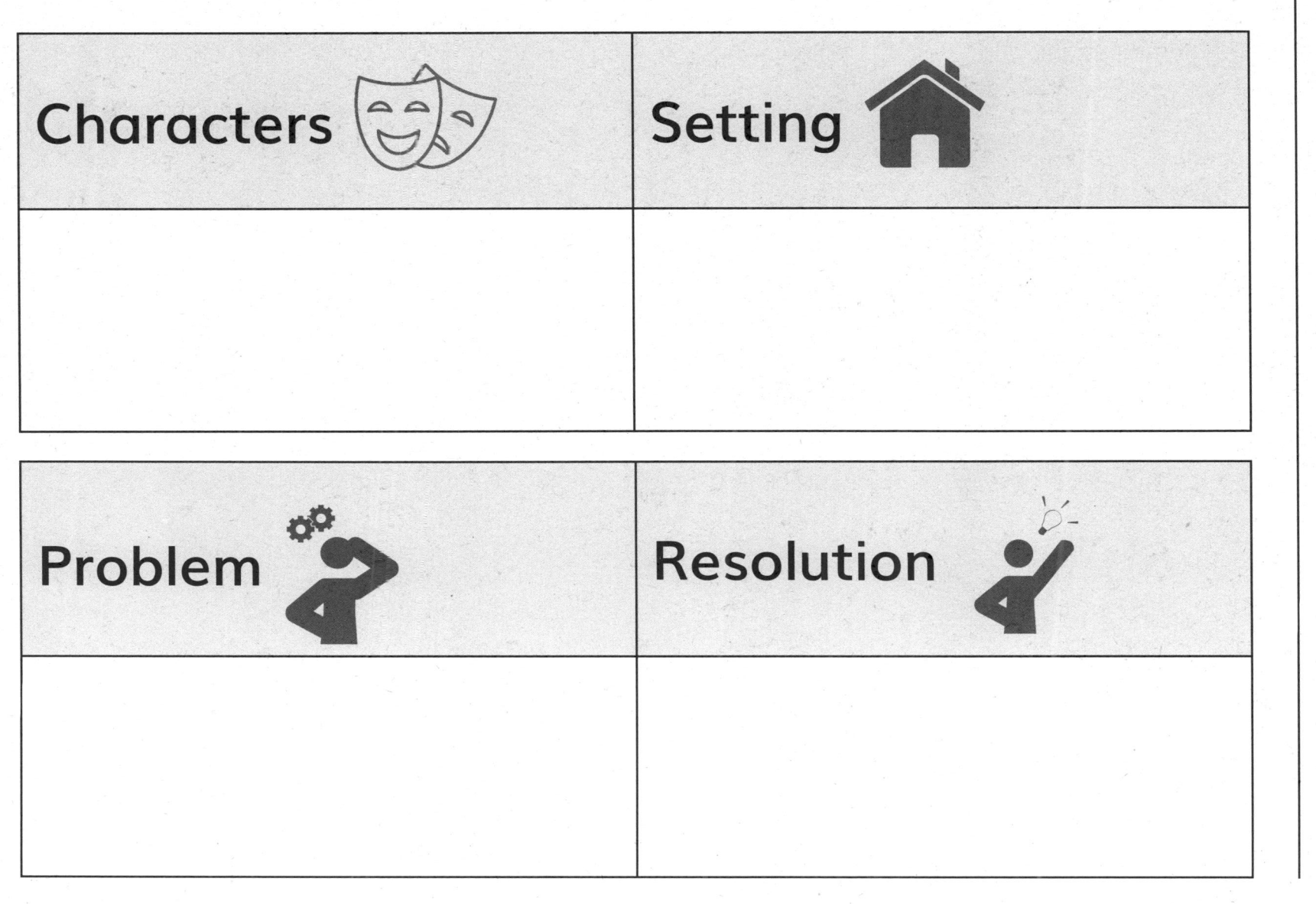

Handout 18A: Story Map

Directions: Write and illustrate to complete the Story Map for *That Book Woman*.

Setting	
Characters	

Resolution	
Problem	

Name:

Handout 18B: Multiple-Meaning Words

Directions: Draw or write two different definitions for each word.

remote	1	2
poke	3	4
spell	5	6
signs	7	8
duck	9	10

Name:

Handout 19A: Frayer Model

Directions: Fill in the information about the word *scholar* on the Frayer Model.

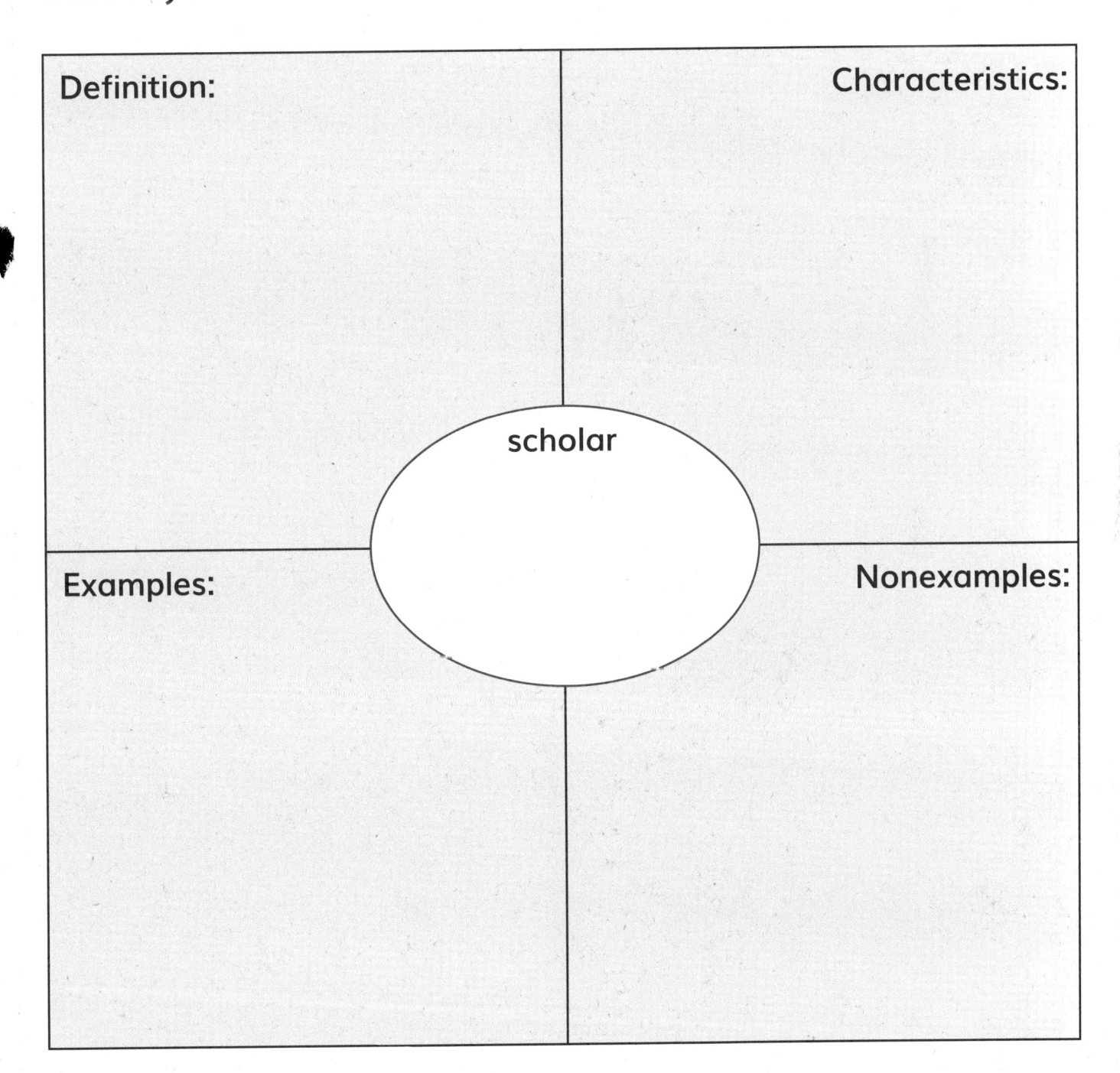

Definition:	Characteristics:
Examples:	Nonexamples:

scholar

Name:

Handout 21A: Focusing Question Task 4

Directions: Write and draw to retell the story *That Book Woman*.

Be sure to include:

-  Characters
- Setting
-  Problem
-  Resolution
- Complete sentences.

Name:

- Capitalized first words in a sentence and proper nouns.

- End punctuation.

- A drawing of Cal, Lark, and the Book Woman, and one adjective to describe each of them.

Name:

Handout 22A:
Adding Adjectives to Nouns

Directions: Choose an adjective from the Adjective Chart to add to each common noun.

the _____ checkers

the _____ dress

the _____ chickens

the _____ books

Handout 23A: New-Read Story Map

Directions: Write and illustrate to complete the Story Map for *Green Eggs and Ham*.

Characters	Setting

Problem	Resolution

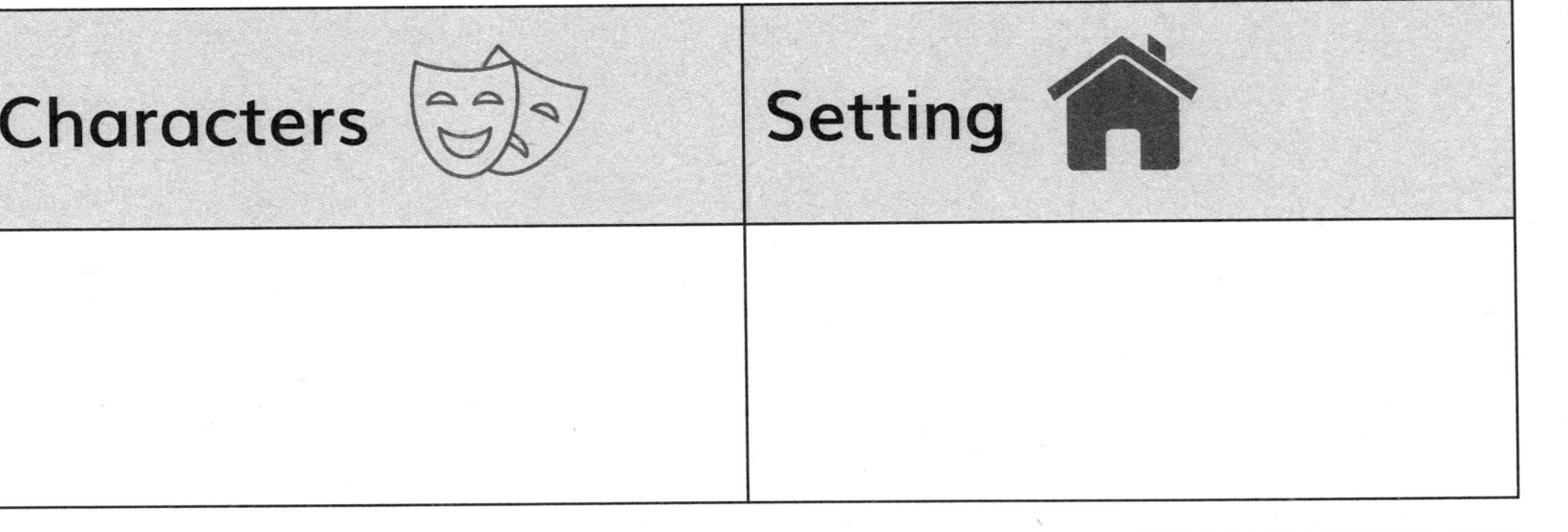

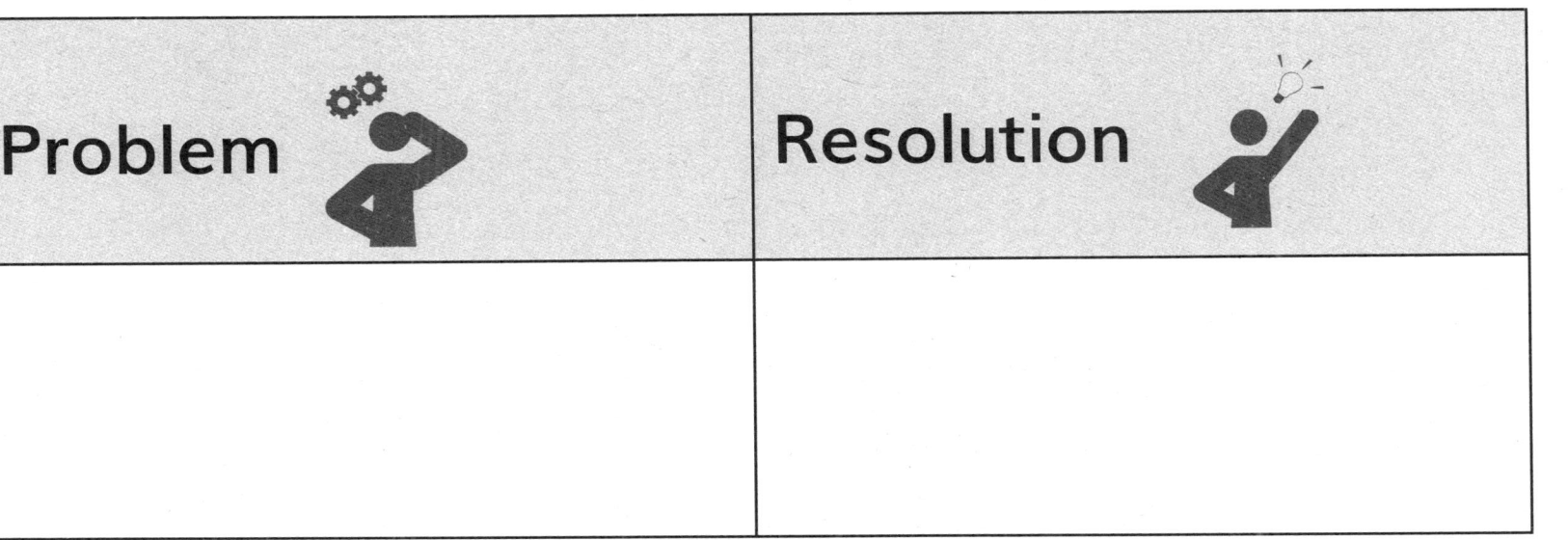

Handout 23B: Fluency Homework

Directions: Have an adult initial each day that you read the passage three to five times. Optional: Have a peer sign on the second row of boxes, checking your progress below.

You do not like them.
So you say.
Try them! Try them!
And you may.
Try them and you may, I say.

Sam!
If you will let me be,
I will try them.
You will see.

I do so like
green eggs and ham!
Thank you!
Thank you,
Sam-I-am!

49 words

Geisel, Theodor Seuss. *Green Eggs and Ham*. G.P. Random House, 1960.

Name:

Day 1	Day 2	Day 3	Day 4

Student Performance Checklist:

- Read easily without stumbling.

- Read with appropriate phrasing and pausing.

- Read with appropriate expression for the selection.

- Read at a good pace, not too fast and not too slow.

- Read to be heard and understood.

Teacher Notes:

Name: _____

Handout 23C: Mixed Sentences

Directions: Read each sentence and circle the sentences that are interrogative.

- Why does Sam-I-am always appear?

- The main character is quite grumpy.

- Just try them already!

- Green eggs and ham look delicious to me.

- Where did the fox come from?

Name:

Handout 24A: Art Vocabulary

Directions: Use the graphic organizers to record text evidence of *portrait*, *landscape*, and *still life*.

Page: _____ is for _____

Page: _____ is for _____

Page: _____ is for _____

Name:

Handout 25A: Sequenced Sentences

Directions: Cut apart the time order word cards. Place the correct word card at the beginning of each sentence.

First	Next	Last
Finally	It all started when	Then

Sam did not like green eggs and ham.

Sam tried green eggs and ham.

Sam liked green eggs and ham.

Name:

Handout 25B: Mixed Sentences

Directions: Read each sentence and circle the sentences that are imperative.

- Why did Sam-I-am go on the boat?

- Dr. Seuss is a great author.

- Finish your breakfast!

- The goat looks hungry.

- Don't just stand there!

Name:

Handout 26A: Focusing Question Task 5

Directions: Write and draw to retell the story *Green Eggs and Ham*.

Be sure to include:

- Characters
- Setting
- Problem
- Resolution
- Time order words.

Name:

- Complete sentences.

- Capital letters at the beginning of a sentence and proper nouns.

- End punctuation.

- An adjective to describe a noun.

Handout 28A: End-of-Module Task

Directions: Write and draw to retell a narrative about a character whose life has changed because of books.

Be sure to include:

- Characters

- Setting

- Problem

- Resolution

- Complete sentences that begin with a capital letter and end with a punctuation mark.

Name:

- Capitals at the beginning of proper nouns.

- Illustrations to match the words on each page.

Use your best handwriting, as you will read and share your story with your classmates and teacher.

Name: _____

Handout 28B: Fluency Homework

Directions: Have an adult initial each day that you read the poem three to five times. Optional: Have a peer sign on the second row of boxes, checking your progress below.

"Museum AB—See!"

"A is for Apple"—I see red, green, gold.
"B is for Boat"—I see lines so bold!
"C is for Cat"—I see fuzzy friends.
"D is for Dance"—I see leaps and bends.
"E is for Egg"—I see ovals round.
"F is for Feet"—I see toes on the ground.
"G is for Game"—I see people play.
"H is for Hair"—I see curls of gray.
"I is for Insect"—I see bees that sting.
"J is for Jewelry"—I see a gold ring.
"K is for Kiss"—I see love and care.
"L is for Light"—I see fires flare.
"M is for Monster"—Wait! What did you say?
See you later! I'm done for the day!

111 Words

Adapted from The Metropolitan Museum of Art. *Museum ABC*. Little, Brown Books for Young Readers, 2002.

Name:

Day 1	Day 2	Day 3	Day 4

Student Performance Checklist:

- Read easily without stumbling.

- Read with appropriate phrasing and pausing.

- Read with appropriate expression for the selection.

- Read at a good pace, not too fast and not too slow.

- Read to be heard and understood.

Teacher Notes:

Name:

Handout 29A: Narrative Checklist

Directions: Use the checklist to revise and edit your narrative.

Reading Comprehension	Self	Peer
I understand how people around the world get books.	😐 😊	😐 😊

Structure		
I have characters.	😐 😊	😐 😊
I have a setting.	😐 😊	😐 😊
I have a problem.	😐 😊	😐 😊
I have a resolution.	😐 😊	😐 😊

Conventions		
I use end punctuation. . ? !	😐 😊	😐 😊
I write complete sentences.	😐 😊	😐 😊

Name: _____

Handout 32A:
Socratic Seminar Self-Reflection

Directions: Evaluate your participation in the Socratic Seminar by writing an A, S, or N in the chart below.

A = I always did that.
S = I sometimes did that.
N = I'll do that next time.

Expectation	Evaluation (A, S, N)
I followed our class's rules for the seminar.	
I responded to what others said at least once.	
I noticed pauses.	
I listened with my whole body.	

Name: _____

Read Aloud

A World of Books, Grade 1, Module 1

Directions: Share what you know about the importance of books and reading by sharing the answers to one question in each category (Wonder, Organize, Reveal, Distill, Know) below. Draw, write, or tell your teacher your answers.

Student Name:

Text:

Author:

Topic:

Genre/type of book:

1. Wonder: Why did you choose this book? What grabbed your attention about the cover or illustrations in the book? Write a sentence or draw a picture showing why you chose it.

Name:

2. **Wonder:** What kind of details do you notice in the illustrations? When you think about the details you found, what do you wonder about the pictures?

3. **Organize:** Who is the book mostly about? What is the main character's biggest problem? How does life change for that character?

4. **Organize:** How does the main character's attitude toward books or reading change from the beginning of the story to the end of the story? Answer using these Sentence Frames:

    a. In the beginning _____.

    b. In the middle _____.

    c. In the end _____.

5. **Reveal:** How does the author show us that books can change lives? Find a page in the book where the author shows that books are important.

Name: _____

6. Reveal: How does the author want us to know about books? Draw a picture that explains one way the author shows or tells us that books can be joyful.

7. Distill: What is the most important idea about books that you learned by reading this story? Draw a picture showing this idea and explain your drawing on the paper or to your teacher.

8. Distill: What new idea about books did you learn from reading this story? Draw a picture showing this important lesson.

9. Know: How does this story connect to the other stories you have read in class about the importance of books and reading?

10. Know: What is an idea that you think kids and adults should know about why books are important and valuable?

G1 > M1 > WIT & WISDOM®

WIT & WISDOM FAMILY TIP SHEET

WHAT IS MY FIRST GRADE STUDENT LEARNING IN MODULE 1?

Wit & Wisdom is our English curriculum. It builds knowledge of key topics in history, science, and literature through the study of excellent texts. By reading and responding to stories and nonfiction texts, we will build knowledge of the following topics:

Module 1: A World of Books

Module 2: Creature Features

Module 3: Powerful Forces

Module 4: Cinderella Stories

In this first module, *A World of Books*, we will study the power of books and libraries around the world. Some people have climbed mountains just to find books. Others have trekked to libraries on boats or even on elephants. In this module, we will ask the question: *How do books—and the knowledge they bring—change lives around the world?*

OUR CLASS WILL READ THESE BOOKS:

Picture Books (Informational)

- *Museum ABC*, The Metropolitan Museum of Art
- *My Librarian Is a Camel*, Margriet Ruurs

Picture Books (Literary)

- *Tomás and the Library Lady*, Pat Mora and Raul Colon
- *Waiting for the Biblioburro*, Monica Brown and John Parra
- *That Book Woman*, Heather Henson and David Small
- *Green Eggs and Ham*, Dr. Seuss

OUR CLASS WILL WATCH THESE VIDEOS:

- "Biblioburro: The Donkey Library," Ebonne Ruffins, CNN
- "Pack Horse Librarians," SLIS Storytelling

OUR CLASS WILL EXAMINE THIS PAINTING:

- *The Midnight Ride of Paul Revere*, Grant Wood

© Great Minds PBC

OUR CLASS WILL ASK THESE QUESTIONS:

- How do library books change life for Tomás?
- How does the Biblioburro change life for Ana?
- How do people around the world get books?
- How does the packhorse librarian change life for Cal?
- How do books change my life?

QUESTIONS TO ASK AT HOME:

As you read with your first grade student, ask:

- *What do you notice and wonder?*

BOOKS TO READ AT HOME:

- *Poppleton*, Cynthia Rylant
- *Rain School*, James Rumford
- *Library Lion*, Michelle Knudsen
- *Abe Lincoln: The Boy Who Loved Books*, Kay Winters and Nancy Carpenter
- *Biblioburro: A True Story from Columbia*, Jeanette Winter
- *The Stone Lion*, Margaret Wild
- *You Wouldn't Want to Live Without Books!*, Alex Woolf
- *Thank You, Mr. Falker*, Patricia Polacco
- *Wild about Books*, Judy Sierra
- *The Library*, Sarah Stewart

PLACES YOU CAN VISIT TO TALK ABOUT BOOKS:

Visit the local library together. Ask the librarian:

- *What is the history of the library?*
- *When was the library built?*
- *Who built the library?*
- *How many people visit the library each year?*
- *What programs does the library offer?*

CREDITS

Great Minds® has made every effort to obtain permission for the reprinting of all copyrighted material. If any owner of copyrighted material is not acknowledged herein, please contact Great Minds® for proper acknowledgment in all future editions and reprints of this module.

- All material from the *Common Core State Standards for English Language Arts & Literacy in History/Social Studies, Science, and Technical Subjects* © Copyright 2010 National Governors Association Center for Best Practices and Council of Chief State School Officers. All rights reserved.

- All images are used under license from Shutterstock.com unless otherwise noted.

- For updated credit information, please visit **http://witeng.link/credits**.

ACKNOWLEDGMENTS

Great Minds® Staff

The following writers, editors, reviewers, and support staff contributed to the development of this curriculum.

Karen Aleo, Elizabeth Bailey, Ashley Bessicks, Sarah Brenner, Ann Brigham, Catherine Cafferty, Sheila Byrd-Carmichael, Lauren Chapalee, Emily Climer, Rebecca Cohen, Elaine Collins, Julia Dantchev, Beverly Davis, Shana Dinner de Vaca, Kristy Ellis, Moira Clarkin Evans, Marty Gephart, Mamie Goodson, Nora Graham, Lindsay Griffith, Lorraine Griffith, Christina Gonzalez, Emily Gula, Brenna Haffner, Joanna Hawkins, Elizabeth Haydel, Sarah Henchey, Trish Huerster, Ashley Hymel, Carol Jago, Mica Jochim, Jennifer Johnson, Mason Judy, Sara Judy, Lior Klirs, Shelly Knupp, Liana Krissoff, Sarah Kushner, Suzanne Lauchaire, Diana Leddy, David Liben, Farren Liben, Brittany Lowe, Whitney Lyle, Stephanie Kane-Mainier, Liz Manolis, Jennifer Marin, Audrey Mastroleo, Maya Marquez, Susannah Maynard, Cathy McGath, Emily McKean, Andrea Minich, Rebecca Moore, Lynne Munson, Carol Paiva, Michelle Palmieri, Tricia Parker, Marya Myers Parr, Meredith Phillips, Eden Plantz, Shilpa Raman, Rachel Rooney, Jennifer Ruppel, Julie Sawyer-Wood, Nicole Shivers, Danielle Shylit, Rachel Stack, Amelia Swabb, Vicki Taylor, Melissa Thomson, Lindsay Tomlinson, Tsianina Tovar, Sarah Turnage, Melissa Vail, Keenan Walsh, Michelle Warner, Julia Wasson, Katie Waters, Sarah Webb, Lynn Welch, Yvonne Guerrero Welch, Amy Wierzbicki, Margaret Wilson, Sarah Woodard, Lynn Woods, and Rachel Zindler

Colleagues and Contributors

We are grateful for the many educators, writers, and subject-matter experts who made this program possible.

David Abel, Robin Agurkis, Sarah Ambrose, Rebeca Barroso, Julianne Barto, Amy Benjamin, Andrew Biemiller, Charlotte Boucher, Adam Cardais, Eric Carey, Jessica Carloni, Dawn Cavalieri, Janine Cody, Tequila Cornelious, David Cummings, Matt Davis, Thomas Easterling, Jeanette Edelstein, Sandra Engleman, Charles Fischer, Kath Gibbs, Natalie Goldstein, Laurie Gonsoulin, Dennis Hamel, Kristen Hayes, Steve Hettleman, Cara Hoppe, Libby Howard, Gail Kearns, Lisa King, Sarah Kopec, Andrew Krepp, Shannon Last, Ted MacInnis, Christina Martire, Alisha McCarthy, Cindy Medici, Brian Methe, Ivonne Mercado, Patricia Mickelberry, Jane Miller, Cathy Newton, Turi Nilsson, Julie Norris, Tara O'Hare, Galemarie Ola, Tamara Otto, Christine Palmtag, Dave Powers, Jeff Robinson, Karen Rollhauser, Tonya Romayne, Emmet Rosenfeld, Mike Russoniello, Deborah Samley, Casey Schultz, Renee Simpson, Rebecca Sklepovich, Kim Taylor, Tracy Vigliotti, Charmaine Whitman, Glenda Wisenburn-Burke, and Howard Yaffe

Early Adopters

The following early adopters provided invaluable insight and guidance for Wit & Wisdom:

- Bourbonnais School District 53 • Bourbonnais, IL
- Coney Island Prep Middle School • Brooklyn, NY
- Gate City Charter School for the Arts • Merrimack, NH
- Hebrew Academy for Special Children • Brooklyn, NY
- Paris Independent Schools • Paris, KY
- Saydel Community School District • Saydel, IA
- Strive Collegiate Academy • Nashville, TN
- Valiente College Preparatory Charter School • South Gate, CA
- Voyageur Academy • Detroit, MI

Design Direction provided by Alton Creative, Inc.

Project management support, production design and copyediting services provided by ScribeConcepts.com

Copyediting services provided by Fine Lines Editing

Product management support provided by Sandhill Consulting